A Gushing Rock

: Isaiah 48:21-22 : They did not thirst when He Led them through the deserts. He made the water flow out of the Rock for them; He split the Rock and water gushed forth. "There is no peace for he wicked" says the LORD.

The God of all creation's provision for humanity. The Gushing Rock, our Redeemer

Ken Joo Cor Temple's Discipleship handbook , meant for the Family of Ken Joo Cor to recall basic training and concepts around the Globe.

By: Rav (pastor) Nelson Cortes II, D,Min.   -Dedicated to KJCT Family

While we were still sinners Messiah died for us, for our Redemption by faith and charity

Welcome to **the Ken Joo Cor Temple** family disciples of the **Holy One of Israel**.

This discipleship manual in no way supersedes the authority of the written Infallible Word of God.

The Tanakh (OT) and B'rit Hadashah (NT) composed of 66 books completes our Cannon or Holy Scriptures.

We put our faith in the God of the Bible, and trust and know that He has given us a new heart or nature. Enlightenment or Regeneration comes from hearing the Word of God, and His goodness leads us to redemption from total depravity. Giving meaning to life or social constructs for the benefit of Liberty and Justice for all.

Verified Text :

1. Complete Jewish Bible (CJB) by David Stern

2.Authorized 1611 King James Bible

3.Casiodoro de Reina (1569)- revised by Cipriano de Valera (1602) up to 1909, Spanish Bible Reina-Valera edition.

4.NASB 1995- for Children

5. Arabic Bible, Translated by Smith & Van Dyke, 1865.

Psalm 144 King James Version (KJV)

Blessed be the LORD my strength which teacheth my hands to war, and my fingers to fight:
2 My goodness, and my fortress; my high tower, and my deliverer; my shield, and he in whom I trust; who subdueth my people under me.
3 LORD, what is man, that thou takest knowledge of him! or the son of man, that thou makest account of him!
4 Man is like to vanity: his days are as a shadow that passeth away.
5 Bow thy heavens, O LORD, and come down: touch the mountains, and they shall smoke.
6 Cast forth lightning, and scatter them: shoot out thine arrows, and destroy them.
7 Send thine hand from above; rid me, and deliver me out of great waters, from the hand of strange children;
8 Whose mouth speaketh vanity, and their right hand is a right hand of falsehood.
9 I will sing a new song unto thee, O God: upon a psaltery and an instrument of ten strings will I sing praises unto thee.
10 It is he that giveth salvation unto kings: who delivereth David his servant from the hurtful sword.
11 Rid me, and deliver me from the hand of strange children, whose mouth speaketh vanity, and their right hand is a right hand of falsehood:
12 That our sons may be as plants grown up in their youth; that our daughters may be as corner stones, polished after the similitude of a palace:
13 That our garners may be full, affording all manner of store: that our sheep may bring forth thousands and ten thousands in our streets:

¹⁴ That our oxen may be strong to labour; that there be no breaking in, nor going out; that there be no complaining in our streets.
¹⁵ Happy is that people, that is in such a case: yea, happy is that people, whose God is the LORD.

We follow Christ as our Lord and Savior. The only mediator between Man and God.

Isaiah 7, 9, 10:21 Born of Virgin, Mighty God, and Everlasting Father. Acts 5 Don't lie to Holy Ghost

We are not Judiazers; meaning the just shall live by faith. Each person has their own measure of faith (personal conviction) or unique ministry (obligation) or vocation in life and the right to worship according to Scripture and the Liberty in Christ. Romans 14 - Let each be convinced in their own mind, although no Scripture is open to private interpretation 2 Peter 1:20. Also know that Christ came to fulfill the law (meet it's requirements as an example) not destroy the Law of God. Matt 5:17-20 should be memorized throughout the foundation of your training.

We do believe in Torah and Pentecost, the 10 commandments found in Exodus 20 and shall not shun from the full council of God from Genesis to Revelation, but are respectful of our Jewish brethren who only believe in the Tanahk, for the gentile church is grafted in through the Messiah and must pray for those who guard the Oracles of God. Romans 9-12 will address this and Corinthians, Galatians

We believe in Levitcus 23 being the only major Biblical Holidays, Passover ,Resurrection Day and Sukkot or Feast of Booths.

Easter and Christmas are both pagan compromises, even the Puritan church didn't celebrate Christmas

Jesus was born Oct 6, Six months after his cousin John the Baptist - Thus Sukkot or Emmanuel "God with us" was Oct 6 of that specific year due to Zacharias the Priest allowing us to calculate the timing (Luke 1). Due to the Lunar Hebrew Calendar Sukkot changes like the American Holiday Thanksgiving 1863.

* Recall that the Hebrew Calendar doesn't add the 10 days that were introduced by Pope Gregory XIII known as the Gregorian Reformation, which lead to some wanting a Oct 15th birth, so then they also try to take that point to December 15, which is way over 6 months from March when Elizabeth waited to visit Mary.

Warning! Results for year 1752 C.E. and earlier may be inaccurate.
Hebrew calendar does not take into account a correction of ten days that was introduced by Pope Gregory XIII known as the Gregorian Reformation.[1]

These are finer points of Theology (the meat of the Word) and we must continue to stand in unity and trust in the Feast of Tabernacle as being the birth reference and Celebration.

Isaiah 5:20 - Woe unto them that call evil good, and good evil; that put darkness for light, and light for darkness; that put bitter for sweet, and sweet for bitter!

*This is why the (KJCT) Ken Joo Cor Temple doesn't recognize Christmas since the Puritan Church had outlawed the practice until former General , then President Ulysses Grant made the Winter Solstice (christmas) a national holiday after the American railroad was completed. Recall Daniel's warning of the end of days Knowledge and travel will excel, and continue.

also the Puritan church celebrated Sukkot in 1621 which later became Thanksgiving 1863

Second, we don't recognize the false sexual goddess of fertility Easter or , cognate with modern Dutch *ooster* and German *Ostern*, developed from an Old English word that usually appears in the form *Ēastrun, -on,* or *-an*; but also as *Ēastru, -o*; and *Ēastre* or *Ēostre*. The most widely accepted theory of the origin of the term is that it is derived from the name of a goddess mentioned by the 7th to 8th-century English monk Bede, who wrote that *Ēosturmōnaþ* (Old English 'Month of Ēostre', translated in Bede's time as "Paschal month") was an English month, corresponding to April, which he says "was once called after a goddess of theirs named Ēostre, in whose honour feasts were celebrated in that month". However, it is possible that Bede was only speculating about the origin of the term since there is no firm evidence that such a goddess actually existed.

We celebrate Passover and Resurrection Day in remembrance our of deliverance and salvation paid for by God himself. As John the Baptist announced Christ "The Lamb of the world" for those who believe.

Science isn't a Religion, it's a tool used to understand the laws of nature. These fact's contrived by the scientific method shouldn't change due them being justified by repeated testing.

Early scientist like Galileo and Sir Issac Newton used the Bible as researched and corrected false theology or man-made ideologies, such as the Earth being the center of the universe.

Cosmological Science or Origin science has accepted a valid theory called "Intelligent Design" or (ID)

Sadly, Today our public education system continue to be biases towards Darwin's Evolution Theory as the final solution without even offering to propose ID theory to the general population.

Basically, in short when we look at a painting one must and can logically concluded that someone painted it. Whether it's a copy or original is besides the point, this lead us to discuss that their must be One-all powerful, yet loving Creator of the Universe and were not just some product of the Sci-Fi thriller the Matrix.

Absolute nothing, can't produce anything - meaning the Big bang couldn't just have started itself. That would be out of logical constructs and thus self defeating. Therefore their must be One Supreme being known as God and no other's or else that would destroy the definition of what is God.

The Universe is not Eternal - The second law of Thermodynamics called "Entropy" proves that even the Universe is not everlasting only God's word; proof would be a SuperNova what the destruction of a star.

Therefore the Big-Bang Theory couldn't start itself. Absolute nothing, can't produce even a spark in pitch darkness. This is logical proof to be a theist (believer in God) unlike Siddhartha Gautama or (Buddha) was an Atheist coming from a Polytheist society crossing the Himalayas, who taught the Universe was eternal.

Origin of Buddhism born **562 BCE or 480 BCE** and **died 483 BCE or 400 BCE** to around age 80

Entropy - is a fact of nature and thus Buddhism is self-defeating but with Love and respect with honor other journey to God for Romans 1:19-21 states " because that which is known about God is evident within them; for God made it evident to them. [20] For since the creation of the world His invisible attributes, His eternal power and divine nature, have been clearly seen, being understood through what has been made, so that they are without excuse. [21] For even though they knew God, they did not honor Him as God or give thanks, but they became futile in their speculations, and their foolish heart was darkened."

I'm grateful for Eastern medicine, since it's similar to Biblical medicine rather than western socialism derived from Eugenics or modern day anthropology such vaccination for population control.

Most credit Hippocrates for "Let food be thy medicine and medicine be thy food." 460- 370.BC

Ezekiel 47:12 - NASB "By the river on its bank, on one side and on the other, will grow all kinds of trees for food Their leaves will not wither and their fruit will not fail They will bear every month because their water flows from the sanctuary, and their fruit will be for food and their leaves for healing." **593-571 BC.**

In 2017 ce, according to the Jewish Calendar it's currently 5777 meaning our Religion has been recorded since 3760 BCE

The only major world power prior to Abraham hearing his call from God would be the Egyptians and Babylonian Empire which were both polytheistic cultures. Polytheists are also self defeating, thus destroying the attributes of the Supreme being. These pagan deities all required human sacrifice at one point, but in Judeo-Christianity God provides Himself and allows us to be reconciled by faith in His own sacrifice and not trusting in our merit to earn salvation .

Romans 16:1-7 NASB - Written circa 50-55 AD, or BCE

I commend to you our sister Phoebe, who is a [a]servant of the church which is at Cenchrea; ²that you receive her in the Lord in a manner worthy of the [b]saints, and that you help her in whatever matter she may have need of you; for she herself has also been a helper of many, [c]and of myself as well.
³Greet Prisca and Aquila, my fellow workers in Christ Jesus, ⁴who for my life risked their own necks, to whom not only do I give thanks, but also all the churches of the Gentiles; ⁵also *greet* the church that is in their house. Greet Epaenetus, my beloved, who is the first convert to Christ from **Asia**. ⁶Greet Mary, who has worked hard for you. ⁷Greet Andronicus and Junias, my kinsmen and my fellow prisoners, who are outstanding among the apostles, who also were in Christ before me.

*The early church spread the Truth of the Gospel sealed by their own blood, why lie about a resurrection of our Messiah just to die? These were eyewitness to the risen Christ, compared to being a Muslim martyr for 70+ virgins.

Christianity, Shaolin Buddhism, and the Tang dynasties , 6th and 7th centuries - Christians and Buddhist can live civilly and allow each other to worship freely. Unlike a sincere Islamic follower of Mohammad or Allah (the false god of War aka Satan) , I'm not referring to those who are culturally born into the Muslim world, but the Terrorist Islam which was formed September 622 AD or BCE by Mohammad (Anti-Semitic) Genesis 12: All nations will be blessed or cursed accordingly to their position against God and his people .

Know your enemies attitude against other civilizations, they know the home is the first Church and are breaking down the nuclear family structure.

Quran 3:28 - states below:

Let not the believers take the disbelievers as Auliya (supporters, helpers, etc.) instead of the believers, and whoever does that will never be helped by God in any way, except if you indeed fear a danger from them. And God warns you against Himself (His Punishment), and to God is the final return. Qur'an 3:28

Surah 5:51, 3:28 and 4:144 says that it refers to those people who aim to harm Muslims or mock, and Insult Islam and Muslims should not be friends with these people.

Ibn Kathir's (1301 – 1373 AD) commentary on 5:51, he explains in more detail elsewhere who these individuals are referred to in 5:51. He states that the verse refers to those who mock, insult Islam and harm, persecute and expel Muslims. That a Muslim is forbidden from befriending such a people:

Shaolin Temple was formed by Batvo from 495-520 CE, AD
Then handed down to Boddhidharmarma 527-540 and this custom of reincarnation has been passed down all the way to Shi YONGXIN born 1987- and current Abbot.

On 6/4/2000 AD - Charles Mattera and Steve DeMasco both changed thier names and became disciple of the Abbot

<u>Announcements from the Shaolin Temple</u>

Shihan Paul Taylor - who studied under Charles Mattera since he was 10 was removed from the monument at the Shaolin Temple in China.
"In a show of support for The United Studios of Self Defense, Inc. the Shaolin Temple has forever removed Paul Taylor's name from the USSD temple monument dedicated in 2004.

On 7-3-11, Wang Yu Min, spokesperson for the Shaolin Temple state that Paul has betrayed our disciple, Yan Deng (Professor Mattera), considering this betrayal as shameful behavior."
Then the following day, the same spokesperson from the Shaolin Temple on 7-4-11 he stated
"The Shaolin Temple supports United Studios of Self Defense Inc. and it's battle against Z-Ultimate. The Temple stands for loyalty and honor... and does not support treachery and bad behavior. United Studios and the Shaolin Temple are one!"

<u>Thus each of these studios now and have always promoted Buddhism as it's main philosophy and has ties to Hinduism.</u>

Z-Ultimate's Self defense response was to ally itself with other sectors of Chinese monastery, which are found in the Wudang Mountains and are considered Taoist also known as Daoism in worldview.

Taoism differs from Confucianism by not emphasizing rigid rituals and social order.[1] Taoist ethics vary depending on the particular school, but in general tend to emphasize wu wei (effortless action), "naturalness", simplicity, spontaneity, and the Three Treasures: 慈 "compassion", 儉 "frugality", and 不敢為天下先 "humility",

The roots of Taoism go back at least to the 4th century BCE. Early Taoism drew its cosmological notions from the School of Yin-yang (Naturalists), and was deeply influenced by one of the oldest texts of Chinese culture, the *Yijing*, which expounds a philosophical system about how to keep human behavior in accordance with the alternating cycles of nature.

Thus leading Z-Ultimate to be an extension of the Taoist Temple. They claim to be more traditional from the Han dynasty saying that they are the origin of Chinese Martial arts, which then lead to the rest of modern Karate. Since lack of Tibetan influence they worship Xuanwu in WaDang as the Dark Warlord.

Prior to all this in the 1960's Charles Mattera was a student of Fred Villari who was his original instructor

---

2016 A.D , CE - Ken Joo Cor Temple established.

Christ is our foundation cornerstone, and head of our Temple

Rav. Cortes and the Ken Joo Cor Temple (KJCT) family are glad to present to you and your loved one's a balanced Martial Art for ages 4+. This 7 belt ranking art is designed to prepare you for your daily life, and provided a Christian Worldview. There is no need to study beyond a Black Belt in our organization unless your called to be a Pastor or Lord willing a Rav.

Having studied The Holy Bible for years; I dedicated my life to serving God. Then in 2012, known as Carmageddon 2, the second closure of the 405 fwy in Los Angeles, Rav. Cortes was rear-end with a sea of red brake lights ahead. This was Sept. 29th 2012, heading northbound on 5 FWY near Dodger Stadium near the S-bend in the FWY. The collision ripped 4 Spinal Disc in the Lumbar alone, and also injured midback and neck. Through Chiropractic Care and Acupuncture disc L2 and L3 healed over the course of a few years, but L4 and L5 needed surgical intervention bilaterally due to unstable blood pressure due to having an instable pelvis causing extreme pressure on the 10th Cranial nerve known as "Vagus nerve".

Bruce Lee had injured only his L4 disc and was told he would never be able to walk again without assistance or kick again. After 4 years of agony; the surgery was necessary to prevent a stroke basically a brain hemorrhage which is what Bruce Lee died from at 32. It wasn't an allergic reaction to medicine, probably lack of proper pain management led to his death. Once injured Bruce suffered the rest of his life, even using stunt doubles for jumping scenes in his films to protect his back. Chronic pain tends to lead to depression or fits of rage due to feeling isolated from the physical pain.

Praise God, after 3 days of being Hospitalized from my surgery on May 5th, 2016 I was released into bed rest for 6 weeks, then intense Physical Therapy began and I could barely move once again; but by the power of God I slowly did my exercises, My doctors were impressed that I was able to self correct myself and really trying. I could not give up, Christ compelled me to continue the struggle of learning to discover my body again. Since being released I've developed and created Ken Joo Cor as style of Martial arts to combat Islamic Terrorism. The Temple promotes a healthy and enjoyable peaceful lifestyle working with my own hands minding my own business.

God has led many key victories in our lives here in the (KJCT) Family, The most grateful is our Salvation. After years of studying and seeking relief, while trusting in our Great Physician I was able to develop this specific style of practical defense for the unexpected in life.

This Judeo-Christian art will increase your confidence and develop a deeper relationship with our loving Eternal Heavenly Father and Creator of all.

Ken : Knowledge in a system.
Joo: Respect for the Oracles of God, Israel, and the elect. The 66 books of the Holy Scriptures from Genesis to Revelation. Consider the book of Isaiah for a moment 66 chapters, sometimes referred to as the mini-Bible reflects the layout of Scripture. Jesus also fulfilled over 300 prophecies regarding to His Diety.

Cor: Christ our Redeemer, 10 Ken Joo's relect the 10 commandments and 7 "Cor" combo's reflect God perfection. Established in 2016, with a rich history of Eldership as seen in Acts 15.

Contact us or Donate to: We are a 501(c) Religious organization and able to give our members a educational or spiritual deductible with every electronic or check donation.

Ken Joo Cor Temple
PO Box 1183
Glendale, CA 91209

www.KenJooCor.com

https://www.facebook.com/nelson.cortes.39545

https://www.facebook.com/KJCTemple

Also: Pray about sponsoring the local youth in single families, or you can tithe to us for the Lord loves a cheerful giver. May the Lord bless you and your loved ones and as you seek His Kingdom of righteousness.

The following content is for disciples of our Temple or congregation in Triune-Godhead. ELOHIM This material is meant to be only a reference once taught to you by your local studio or Temple Instructor.
The reason for this is safety, we want to prevent injuries and be noble citizens here on earth and in Heaven.

---

1 Timothy 3:14-16 CJB (Complete Jewish Bible)

I hope to visit you soon; but I am writing these things 15so that if I am delayed, you may know how one should behave in the household of God, which is the Messianic Community of the living God, the pillar and support of the truth. 16Great beyond all question is the formerly hidden truth underlying our faith:
He was manifested physically
and proved righteous spiritually,
seen by angels
and proclaimed among the nations,
trusted throughout the world
and raised up in glory to heaven.

How to study the Bible word of God:

Context: Who, what, where, when, why? Like any good reporter take your time investigating the Glory of God.

Types of text found within Scriptures
1.Narrative = story or facts
2.Epistle = letter for church edification
3.Parable = story to illustrate (fiction) Luke 19:27
4.Poetry = figurative or symbolic language
5. Prophecy = Future events to unfold, 1/4 of the Bible is fulfilled prophecy

*Extra Biblical proof that Yeshua (Jesus) was a real man can be found in chapter 19, of Roman Historian Flavius Josephus proving that Christ was performing miracles as found written in our Holy Scriptures.

Recall we are all One in Messiah and all equally loved as his children and creation (non-believers). The ranking system in KJCT is only for safety and educational purposes; not meant to over inflate one's ego.

1.White - Form 1 - 10 point blocking
2.Yellow - Form 2 - 10 point blocking with half-step
3.Orange - Form 3 - 10 point blocking with counter-strikes
4.Purple - Form 4 - 10 point blocking with counter and half-steps
5.Blue -   Form 5 - Peaceful River
6.Green   Form 6 - River Rapids
7. Black   Form 7 - Bone Crusher

8. Red - Instructor ,Forms 8 and 9 Etc.

Drills and expected Goals of progress

Spatial Drills
1. Clock (White)
2. Box step (White /yellow)
3. 10 point blocking system (White- Orange)
4. Kicking drills (Orange-Purple)
5. Personal Drills with counter steps (Blue)

Footwork Drills
1. Pivot to the rear (white)

2.Shuffle Drills(Yellow- Orange)

3.Cross over drills (Orange)

4. 30/70 stance drills(Orange)

5. Sweep drills(Blue)

6. Leg reap & hock (leg-joint) driils (green) JKT

Civil Defense Drills

1. Line Drills (white)

2. Falling Drills (White-yellow-orange)

3. Roll Drills (purple)

4. Gauntlet (Blue)

5.Conditioning drills (Green)

6. Final versatility (Black)

Sparring Practice

1. 3- step (Yellow)

2.5-step (Orange)

3.Bobbing and weaving (green)

4. Boxing Drill (Black)

Ken Joo # 1. - **Thou shalt have no other gods before me**

1. Begin in the 50/50 stance with hands on guard. As opponent attacks deliver right front ball kick to solar plexus. Cross right foot over left , then step out on guard. - Traditional version. Modified knee, groin

---

Ken Joo # 2. - **Thou shalt not make unto thee any graven images.**

2. This second Ken Joo is simple but effective in a street conflict.

*The length of your leg gives you a reach advantage over assailant arm in most situations. During practice no contact is made. Practice slowly, learning to develop technique over power. Hours of repetition are yours, expect it now and for the rest of your life, but may your exercise never become idolatry for it is better to exercise Godliness; meaning the study of Scriptures should be your primary goal, after you handle all other affairs. One must balance life socially, with a Christian Worldview, and exercise or form.

Begin in 50/50 stance with hands on guard. Avoid opponents attack with left foot towards 9 o'clock chamber your right leg and deliver side blade kick to ribs. Cross right foot over left and stand on gaurd.

Ken Joo #3 - **Thou shalt not take the Lord's name in vain.**

3. Begin in 50/50 stance with hands on guard. As opponent attacks, half-step backward with right foot while executing a left outward #2 block (keep fist closed until Blue) into knife hand, continue with same hand and grab attackers wrist. Right front ball kick to solar plexus and immediately roundhouse ball kick to attackers temple with same foot. Cross right foot over left and get on guard.

Ken Joo #4 - **Remember the Sabbath Day to keep it Holy.**

4. Begin in 50/50 stance with hands on guard. As opponent attacks, half-step backward with right foot while executing left #2 block, keep fist closed until Blue, grab wrist after block with same hand. Right front ball kick to solar plexus and immediately roundhouse ball kick to temple with same leg. Step down bringing your feet together with your right side toward opponent, then deliver a right upward Y strike to opponents wrist, then right side trust kick to ribs. Cross right foot over left and on guard.

Ken Joo #5 - **Honor thy Father and Thy Mother** : also known as "shift change" due to social obligations

5. Begin in 50/50 stance, block with #4, then use momentum from block and spin behind opponents and execute right palm strike to kidney then left middle knuckle strike exposed temple. (Blue +) grab hair if necessary pull back and finish with knife hand to the neck.

Ken Joo #6 - **Thou shalt not kill -** we are defenders of the weak and live for mercy and justice.

6. Begin in 50/50 stance with hands on guard. When opponent punches, box step away yet close enough to 90 degrees perpendicular to your attacker's strike (you should be facing their arm) simultaneously execute #3 Block. Quickly roll your right arm into a back two-knuckle Punch to the chin. Shuffle into or towards opponent and perform horizontal Elbow strike to Solar plexus, Enemy will lose balance, use that to scoop opponents left foot with right hand, then knife hand strike to groin. Pivot right foot back clockwise into Fighting stance.

* In real combat deliver the final strike, while in the studio partner will lie down and no contact. Be sure your partner knows how to fall safely.

Ken Joo #7 - **Thou shall not commit adultery.**

7. Assume 50/50 stance with hand on guard. Avoid opponent's strike leaning and stepping forward and downward at 45 degrees toward 10:30 o'clock, 12 being your front and 6 o'clock means behind you. Then deliver right front two knuckle punch to groin. Grab opponents right shoulder and use "pulley system technique" to twist and turn your enemy by grabbing their right shoulder with your left hand as right rolls up and strikes temple. Reach past enemy head to grab shoulder with right hand simultaneously push with left hand and pull with right , causing attacker to spin towards to you and then the ground as you pivot to 7:30 o'clock. Finish with left front two-knuckle punch to nose

*Do not takedown sparring partner hard until blue belt if health allows.

Ken Joo #8 - **Thou shalt not steal**

8. Begin in 50/50 stance with hands on guard. Half-step back with right foot while executing #5 Block, move enemy's arm in circular motion (clockwise), then rake across the face with right hand Claw strike. -While opponent is stunned, deliver right roundhouse ball kick to sternum, then assumes right over left twist stance as enemy falls. Step out with right foot over attacker on floor (small leap) and land in a low 50/50 stance straddling opponents shoulders. Deliver right front two-knuckle punch to the nose, then left Front two-knuckle punch to nose, right foot sweeps head to side as you step back over opponent, then right Heel kick to temple. Cross right foot in front of left toward 10:30 o'clock. Left foot steps out to on guard position.

*Advance (Blue, Green)
Substitute front two knuckle punches with simultaneous Trigger Fingers to eyes, then middle knuckle strike the temples

Studio etiquette - Partner will fall and cover face with hands at all levels of practice. during this Ken Joo

---

Ken Joo #9- **Thou shalt not bear false witness.**

9. Begin in 50/50 stance with hands on guard. As your enemy approaches you, deliver left front ball kick to solar plexus. As you plant your left foot, turn 180 degrees with your attacker and use the momentum from back spin to execute a right Spinning back kick. Follow through until your right leg come behind you, then step back with hand on guard facing your opponents left side.

*Practice Slowly, learn spatial distance and learn to control amount of force delivered. Note where you place your left leg after initial kick. This will factor the effect or strength of second kick.

Ken Joo #10- **Thou shalt not covet thy neighbor's house, wife or possessions.**

10. Begin in 50/50 stance with hands on guard. Right foot steps back towards the left into a 30/70 stance while executing a left downward circular Parry check similar #8 block, step forward with left foot. Wrap your left arm above and around your attackers elbow joint. Right hand then strikes with a Raking Palm, ending just pass the face, then with same hand quickly execute a right Wrist strike to opponents temple. Use your right leg to hock/sweep enemy's right leg while simultaneously striking throat with Y strike. Maintain your elbow lock as opponent falls, front two-knuckle punch to temple, follow with a rolling knife hand strike to nose.

Christ our Redeemer "Cor" x7 A-G

Date of Writing: The Book of Genesis does not state when it was written. The date of authorship is likely between 1440 and 1400 B.C., between the time Moses led the Israelites out of Egypt and his death.

Genesis 15:11 (CJB) - Complete Jewish Bible
Birds of prey swooped down on the carcasses, <u>but Avram drove them away</u>.

A. Afraid Abraham respected life, was a survivalist, and sensitive to the Power of the Holy Ghost.

a. This Cor begins at yellow rank

Begin in 50/50 stance. Half-step back with right foot, execute #2 block. Grab opponents wrist, execute right front ball lick to solar plexus. Land in right half-step stance and execute right front two-knuckle punch to nose followed by left trust punch to solar plexus.

Matthew 10:28 (KJV) - Messiah states Supreme Moral Judgment:
And fear not them which kill the body, but are not able to kill the soul: but rather fear him which is able to destroy both soul and body in hell.

Cor. B

Bethel (House of God) - Brave to be in the Lord's house

Genesis 35:1-3 (CJB)
God said to Ya'akov, "Get up, go up to Beit-El and live there, and make there an altar to God, who appeared to you when you fled 'Esav your brother." 2Then Ya'akov said to his household and all the others with him, "Get rid of the foreign gods that you have with you, purify yourselves, and put on fresh clothes. 3We're going to move on and go up to Beit-El. There I will build an altar to God, who answered me when I was in such distress and stayed with me wherever I went."

B. God said to Jacob, get up and go to Beth-EL. Jacob was obedience lead to genuine worship or meditation. He turned from idolatry realizing that man-made "gods" were futile. We must conduct an inventory of our priorities and make sure they are in-line with the Fruits of the Spirit of God.

Galatians 5:22-26 (KJV)
    22. But the fruit of the Spirit is love, joy, peace, longsuffering, gentleness, goodness, faith,
    23. Meekness, temperance: against such there is no law.
    24. And they that are Christ's have crucified the flesh with the affections and lusts.
    25. If we live in the Spirit, let us also walk in the Spirit.
    26. Let us not be desirous of vain glory, provoking one another, envying one another.

Begin in 50/50 stance, execute block #2 and grab attackers wrist simultaneously half-step forward (brave) with right foot. Front two-knuckle punch combo, Right then left to solo plexus.

*Advanced then right palm strike to nose, follow through and grab opponents hair control the head and bring downwards into your right rising knee strike to face.

Cor. C

Creation, Corner-step, Christ our foundation Cornerstone - emphasis on Triune-Essence of Godhead.

Genesis 1:1 (KJV)
In the beginning God created the heaven and the earth.

Isaiah 28:16 (CJB)
    therefore here is what *Adonai(Lord) ELOHIM (TRIUNE GODHEAD)* says:
    "Look, I am laying in Tziyon(Zion)
    a tested stone, a costly cornerstone,
    a firm foundation-stone;
    he who trusts will not rush here and there.

As a human Christ was tested, and studied Torah at home and in the synagogues. He read the Scriptures out loud on the Sabbath being glorified by all. His testing can be found in Luke 4, yet he fulfilled over 300+ prophecies written in the Tanakh (OT) confirming his Deity, just as the Gospel's account.

Luke 4:1-4 (KJV)

And Jesus being full of the Holy Ghost returned from Jordan, and was led by the Spirit into the wilderness,

2Being forty days tempted of the devil. And in those days he did eat nothing: and when they were ended, he afterward hungered.

3And the devil said unto him, If thou be the Son of God, command this stone that it be made bread.

4And Jesus answered him, saying, It is written, That man shall not live by bread alone, but by every word of God.

Begin 50/50 stance, as enemy attacks "corner-step" (left foot meets right foot, then right foot steps out parallel from enemy's strike, leaving you in another 50/50 stance facing 9 o'clock. Execute #3 block followed by right circular Hammer fist to groin followed by right back two-knuckle punch to chin.

Cor. D - Dance, Dad, Holy Days

1 Samuel 29:5 (KJV)

Is not this David, of whom they sang one to another in dances, saying, Saul slew his thousands, and David his ten thousands?

-Both Kings of Israel where both tested in battle and war hero's. They displayed faith, courage, while respecting the Anointing of God upon the Eldership. They both accepted God's sovereignty to be the Victor of their battles. They weren't perfect men, only God is perfect but we can glean from their positive attributes or attitude.

Psalm 149:3-4 (NASB)

Let them praise His name with dancing;
Let them sing praises to Him with timbrel and lyre.
4For the LORD takes pleasure in His people;
He will beautify the afflicted ones with salvation.

Ecclesiastes 3:1-15

1There is an appointed time for everything. And there is a time for every event under heaven-
2A time to give birth and a time to die;
A time to plant and a time to uproot what is planted.
3A time to kill and a time to heal;
A time to tear down and a time to build up.
4A time to weep and a time to laugh;
A time to mourn and a time to dance.
5A time to throw stones and a time to gather stones;

A time to embrace and a time to shun embracing.
6A time to search and a time to give up as lost;
A time to keep and a time to throw away.
7A time to tear apart and a time to sew together;
A time to be silent and a time to speak.
8A time to love and a time to hate;
A time for war and a time for peace.
9What profit is there to the worker from that in which he toils? 10I have seen the task which God has given the sons of men with which to occupy themselves.
11He has made everything (beautiful)appropriate in its time. He has also set eternity in their heart, yet so that man will not find out the work which God has done from the beginning even to the end.
12I know that there is nothing better for them than to rejoice and to do good in one's lifetime; 13moreover, that every man who eats and drinks sees good in all his labor-it is the gift of God. 14I know that everything God does will remain forever; there is nothing to add to it and there is nothing to take from it, for God has so worked that men should fear Him. 15That which is has been already and that which will be has already been, for God seeks what has passed by.

We are not murders, but upholders of mercy and justice. Just as a rapid dog must be eliminated for the safety of children, so must be the those who attack Israel or God's Children.

Levitcus 23: 44 (CJB)
Thus Moshe announced to the people of Isra'el the designated times of ADONAI.

Matthew 5:17-20 (KJV)
Think not that I am come to destroy the law, or the prophets: I am not come to destroy, but to fulfil.
18 For verily I say unto you, Till heaven and earth pass, one jot or one tittle shall in no wise pass from the law, till all be fulfilled.
19 Whosoever therefore shall break one of these least commandments, and shall teach men so, he shall be called the least in the kingdom of heaven: but whosoever shall do and teach them, the same shall be called great in the kingdom of heaven.
20 For I say unto you, That except your righteousness shall exceed the righteousness of the scribes and Pharisees, ye shall in no case enter into the kingdom of heaven.

Matthew 8:4 (CJB)
Then Yeshua said to him, "See that you tell no one; but as a testimony to the people, go and let the cohen examine you, and offer the sacrifice that Moshe commanded."

* This proves that the Law of Moses, meant the written Word of God or Himself, thus mainstream Christianity must repent of trying to make Christ exclusive of the Law or Torah. He did what was impossible for humanity, and by faith we have been imputed His righteousness, let's continue walking worthy of that righteous shining forth the Gospel as ambassadors of God Almighty.

D. Begin in 50/50 stance. then step back away from attacker into 30/70 stance (Parry) and execute #2 Block, then grab opponents wrist. Right punch solar plexus, then release left hand and follow through tracing attacker's arm to knife-hand strike the neck, then finish with right leg Stepping Stone kick to sternum or ribs - Traditional version

*Advanced version or modified involves a sweep

Cor E - Exodus 20 review and God's grace, Escape, Eternal Security

1 Corinthians 10:1-4 must be written out by hand on a notebook and notes. Start with NASB, KJV, then CJB version printed.

Now, brothers, I must remind you of the Good News which I proclaimed to you, and which you received, and on which you have taken your stand, 2and by which you are being saved — provided you keep holding fast to the message I proclaimed to you. For if you don't, your trust will have been in vain. 3For among the first things I passed on to you was what I also received, namely this: the Messiah died for our sins, in accordance with what the *Tanakh* says; 4and he was buried; and he was raised on the third day, in accordance with what the *Tanakh* says; 5and he was seen by Kefa, then by the Twelve; 6and afterwards he was seen by more than five hundred brothers at one time, the majority of whom are still alive, though some have died. 7Later he was seen by Ya'akov (James, his half-brother), then by all the emissaries; 8and last of all he was seen by me, even though I was born at the wrong time. 9For I am the least of all the emissaries, unfit to be called an emissary, because I persecuted the Messianic Community of God. 10But by God's grace I am what I am, and his grace towards me was not in vain; on the contrary, I have worked harder than all of them, although it was not I but the grace of God with me. 11 Anyhow, whether I or they, this is what we proclaim, and this is what you believed.

12But if it has been proclaimed that the Messiah has been raised from the dead, how is it that some of you are saying there is no such thing as a resurrection of the dead? 13If there is no resurrection of the dead, then the Messiah has not been raised; 14and if the Messiah has not been raised, then what we have proclaimed is in vain; also your trust is in vain; 15furthermore, we are shown up as false witnesses for God in having testified that God raised up the Messiah, whom he did not raise if it is true that the dead are not raised. 16For if the dead are not raised, then the Messiah has not been raised either; 17and if the Messiah has not been raised, your trust is useless, and you are still in your sins.

John 10 :14-17 (NASB) -Eternal Security from the mouth of God, our Messiah

I am the good shepherd, and I know My own and My own know Me, 15even as the Father knows Me and I know the Father; and I lay down My life for the sheep. 16I have other sheep, which are not of this fold; I must bring them also, and they will hear My voice; and they will become one flock *with* one shepherd. 17For this reason the Father loves Me, because I lay down My life so that I may take it again. 18No one has taken it away from Me, but I lay it down on My own initiative. I have authority to lay it down, and I have authority to take it up again. This commandment I received from My Father."

1 Corinthians 10:12-14 - (NASB) Escape

Therefore let him who thinks he stands take heed that he does not fall. 13No temptation has overtaken you but such as is common to man; and God is faithful, who will not allow you to be tempted beyond what you are able, but with the temptation will provide the way of escape also, so that you will be able to endure it.

14Therefore, my beloved, flee from idolatry.

* The verses above demonstrate the Sovereignty of God and Human responsibility. Yet His, faithfulness towards His children.

Begin in 50/50 stance with hands on guard. As opponent punches, move your feet so you are 90 degrees perpendicular to opponents, facing the striking arm, simultaneously execute left #2 block into (knife-hand block, for advanced) then hold on to attackers wrist. Strike groin with right circular ridge-hand. Wrap opponents right arm above the elbow joint with your left arm. Turn and pull opponent counter-clockwise, striking the neck with knife-hand strike, pivoting 270 degree on right foot, causing opponent to fall. Deliver two knife-hand strike to the heart, then jump to clear attackers arm with your left arm finish with final rolling right knife-hand to heart and yell. Step back on guard.

Cor. F - Fight, Flee, Forward Mentality (critical thinking)

1 Timothy 6:10-12 (KJV)

For the love of money is the root of all evil: which while some coveted after, they have erred from the faith, and pierced themselves through with many sorrows.

11. But thou, O man of God, flee these things; and follow after righteousness, godliness, faith, love, patience, meekness.

12. Fight the good fight of faith, lay hold on eternal life, whereunto thou art also called, and hast professed a good profession before many witnesses.

2 Timothy 1:7 (NASB) -

For God has not given us a spirit of timidity, but of power and love and discipline.

* Application : Sober-mindedness, being able to prioritize and the mind of Christ.

Begin in 50/50 stance with hands on guard. Step right foot over left into a "twist stance" while executing block #5. Simultaneously redirect attacking arm down on left thigh(perpendicular to their thigh), Deliver right Claw rakes from face down to groin, and the vice versa Clawing from groin to face. Large right circular elbow strike to solar plexus. Large Knife-hand to groin. Left leg steps backward causing attacker to fall, then step out on guard.

Cor. G - God's Victory

Ezekiel 18:32 (KJV)
For I have no pleasure in the death of him that dieth, saith the Lord GOD: wherefore turn yourselves, and live ye.

*The heart of God, who requires mercy over sacrifice. Mercy is not weakness, but meekness meaning power under control.

Begin in 50/50 stance with hands on guard. As opponent attacks, step right and lean away at 45 degrees from the punch. Perform block #2 (advance use open hand- blue and up)to wrist. Then use your right Inverted mid-joint punch "paw-shaped" to forearm nerve bundle, then follow through with same arm to strike exposed armpit as right foot steps forward behind opponent. Step left into 50/50 stance, continue turning counter-clockwise and bring your left foot behind opponent and reassume 50/50 stance perpendicular to attacker (assailant), execute Horizontal Elbow strike to floating ribs. Right hand claw grab to groin, and then with the left hand sweep opponent's right leg. Take down opponent hard and finish with large rolling knife-hand strike to groin.

1 Corinthians 15:3-6 NASB: please write out at least 3 times by hand
For I delivered to you as of first importance what I also received, that Christ died for our sins according to the Scriptures,4. and that He was buried, and that He was raised on the third day according to the Scriptures, 5. and that He appeared to Cephas (Peter), then to the twelve. 6. After that He appeared to more than five hundred brethren at one time, most of whom remain until now, but some have fallen asleep

In Conclusion - The Messiah said, your either with in Him by faith or against His heavenly kingdom; this means as Christians will we **not** use violence as way to destroy culture or force people to convert or die such as Islam. We strive to live peacefully with all men even pray for our enemies but not with.

Why does God allow evil? - If there wasn't Satan false kingdom then their wouldn't be sincere meditation or Worship.

Isaiah 1:18 - Come now, and let us reason together, saith the LORD:
though your sins be as scarlet, they shall be as white as snow;
though they be red like crimson, they shall be as wool.

٢٧ليس هو اله امواتٍ بل اله
احياءَ. فانتم اذاً تضُّلون كثيًرا
٢٨فجاءَ واحدٌ من الكتبة
وسمعهم يتحاورون فلما رأى
انهُ اجابهم حسنًا سألهُ ايَّة
وصيَّة هي اوَّل الكلّ.
٢٩فاجابهُ يسوع ان اوَّل كلّ
الوصايا هي إسمَعْ يا اسرائيل.
الربُّ الهنا ربٌّ واحدٌ.
٣٠وتحبُّ الربَّ الهك من كلّ
قلبك ومن كلّ نفسك ومن كلّ
فكرك ومن كلّ قدرتك. هذه هي
الوصيَّة الاولى.
٣١وثانيةٌ مثلها هي تحبُّ
قريبك كنفسك. ليس وصيةٌ

Living Well with

KENJOOCOR

Real Defense

Made in the USA
Middletown, DE
19 March 2022

62756183R00015